APPRENTICESHIP END POINT ASSESSMENT SUCCESS

Customer Service Practitioner EPA SHOWCASE GUIDANCE

Louise Webber
2019

Apprenticeship Course Code ST0072

Louise Webber

DEDICATION

To all the amazing apprentices out there who are achieving their goals through hard work.

INTRODUCTION AND HOW TO USE THIS BOOK

Many apprenticeship students become understandably nervous in the run up to their end point assessment, or as we will call it, EPA.

Being prepared and organised is the best way to overcome these nerves and feel confident in passing this all important assessment.

This book has been designed to cover what most students say is the most difficult part of the Customer Service Practitioner End Point Assessment – The Showcase.

A lot of students tell me that they simply don't know where to start with the showcase.

This book will help you from literally getting started, through to full confidence in handing in a quality showcase document to give your EPA the best possible start.

This guide to the EPA showcase will give you information and guidance on how to prepare, organise, gather and present your showcase in the run up to your end point assessment.

We have also included an overview of the whole EPA process for the Customer Service Practitioner Standard. This guide only covers the showcase element of the EPA as this is the first, and said to be most daunting area of the EPA. The observation and professional discussion are not discussed in this book, but can be found in the prelude to this book, which covers the entire EPA. See the link below.

https://www.amazon.co.uk/Apprenticeship-End-Point-Assessment-Success-ebook/dp/B07H8KDSB8/ref=sr_1_2?ie=UTF8&qid=1549225391&sr=8-2&keywords=louise+webber

OVERVIEW OF THE EPA FOR THE CUSTOMER SERVICE PRACTITIONER APPRENTICESHIP

The aim of the End Point Assessment (EPA) is to ensure that the apprentice has achieved the required levels of knowledge, skills and competence in their role as a customer service practitioner. The end-point assessment is to verify that the standards set have been met in all areas.

A customer service practitioner is required to be able to deliver high quality service and/or products to customers within their organisation. This could include taking customer orders, taking payments, meeting and greeting customers, offering advice and/or support, sales, complaint handling, aftersales or other suitable customer service-based tasks.

Customer service can be delivered face to face, online or at a customer's own premises. It can also include social media.

Customer service practitioners should be able to provide a high level of customer service in line with their organisations standards, procedures and working methods as well as in line with any appropriate regulatory requirements. As a customer service practitioner, first impressions matter and customer service practitioners should be aware that their actions can influence the customers' experience and impression of the organisation they are representing.

In order to fully achieve this apprenticeship, learners are required to:

- Complete their on-programme period of learning and development
- Pass their End Point Assessment
- Obtain a Pass/Distinction as part of the End Point Assessment

The End Point Assessment is made up of three components:

1. Apprentice showcase

2. Practical observation

3. Professional discussion

For each of the three assessment methods, all pass criteria (100%) must be achieved to progress and to complete the apprenticeship programme.

To be awarded a distinction, you must pass all of the pass criteria, plus a percentage of the distinction criteria in each assessment method as outlined in the table below:

Assessment Method	Weighting	Duration	To achieve a pass	To achieve a Distinction
Apprentice Showcase	65%	After a minimum of 12 months on-programme learning	100%	You must meet all of the pass criteria AND 70% of the distinction criteria
Practical Observation	20%	Minimum of 1 hour	100%	You must meet all of the pass criteria AND 80% of the distinction criteria
Professional Discussion	15%	1 hour	100%	You must meet all of the pass criteria AND 75% of the

Normally the apprentice showcase will be sent to the EPA assessment centre first. This is because this can be marked and checked before going through the other areas of the EPA.

It is normal practice for the practical observation to be completed next and then the professional discussion will be the final area to be covered.

The professional discussion is normally left until last so that any areas that were weak, or not seen, in the other elements of the EPA can be discussed and covered off via the discussion.

The professional discussion gives the EPA assessor a final opportunity to find any outstanding evidence to support the apprentice in passing or in reaching a distinction grade.

The EPA for this standard contains 18 sections. To make this easier to break down each section has been labelled according to the letters of the alphabet. The section numbers are for the purpose of this book (and not on the assessment plan) and are there purely to help you to plan for your EPA.

The actual assessment plan does not give alphabetical references to the standards but doing so can help you to organise your work more efficiently and effectively.

Section	Standard	Element of the EPA this will be assessed by
A	Knowing your customers	Professional discussion
B	Understanding the organisation	Apprentice showcase
C	Meeting regulations and legislation	Apprentice showcase
D	Systems and resources	Apprentice showcase
E	Your role and responsibility	Professional discussion
F	Customer experience	Professional discussion

G	Product and service knowledge	Apprentice showcase
H	Interpersonal skills	Observation
I	Communication	Observation
J	influencing skills	Apprentice showcase
K	Personal organisation	Apprentice showcase
L	Dealing with customer conflict and challenge	Apprentice showcase
M	Developing self	Apprentice showcase
N	Being open to feedback	Apprentice showcase
O	Team working	Apprentice showcase
P	Equality – treating all customers as individuals	Observation
Q	Presentation – dress code, professional language	Observation
R	Right first time	Observation

EPA APPRENTICE SHOWCASE

The apprentice showcase is literally a chance for you to showcase, or show off, all the skills and knowledge you have learned during your Customer Service Practitioner apprenticeship.

The apprentice showcase is weighted at a massive 65% of your entire EPA. So, you need to make sure it's good. To achieve a pass, you need to meet 100% of the criteria.

To achieve a distinction, you need to meet all of the pass criteria <u>and</u> 70% of the distinction criteria as well.

Showcase grade summary:

Pass = 100%, Distinction = ALL of the pass marks and 7 out of 10 of the distinction criteria

---

You should begin work on your showcase at the end of your apprenticeship, so in effect, after the 12 months is up.

However, there is nothing stopping you from starting to collate information and evidence in preparation for creating your showcase and this will help to save you time later.

Below is an extract taken from the assessment plan document for the Customer Service Practitioner Standard:

'*The apprentice showcase will be assessed against an externally set brief, written by the assessment organisation, working with employers and other stakeholders, as appropriate, to ensure consistency.*

It is expected that the externally set brief will include elements such as work-based evidence, including customer feedback, recordings, manager statements and witness statements. It will also include evidence from others, such as mid and end of year performance reviews and feedback. It is important to acknowledge that the employer and training provider will work together throughout the on-programme learning, ensuring all learning is consistently applied throughout the apprenticeship and not just at the end point assessment or in the apprentice showcase.

The apprentice will then present to the independent assessor to provide an opportunity for them to interview the apprentice and delve deeper in to the learning and experience. This is to ensure rigor, competence and independence.'

This means the end point assessment organisation that you are working with for your EPA will set specific guidelines on how the showcase is to be delivered. However, all will have similarities in what they ask you to do for your showcase. Make sure to ask your tutor to get as much information as they can from your end point assessment organisation so that you have an exact idea of their requirements.

Gather the following evidence in preparation for collating your showcase. One or two pieces of evidence for each area will give you a good start:

- Feedback from your tutor/assessor
- Witness statements
- Your performance appraisal and performance reviews
- Manager statements
- Recordings of your dealings with customers
- Customer feedback

Note: Whilst your tutor may have observed you at work delivering customer service and written up an observation report, it is recommended that you do not submit this as evidence for your showcase as some EPA centres may not accept this evidence.

You will provide evidence of your skills, knowledge and competency in customer service. You will also need to demonstrate how you have applied your learning and training into work-based tasks. This means that you need to relate what you put in your showcase to your own place of work and job role. I cannot stress enough how important this is. It is your showcase, not 'stuff off the internet' and you need to make it personal.

Remember, as with all three EPA assessment methods, there is an opportunity for pass or distinction grades (and fail, but let's face it, we are seriously looking to avoid even going there).

As an apprentice, you will need to:

- Demonstrate your knowledge and understanding of the principles and practices laid out in the standard and how these are applied in your work role
- Provide evidence to demonstrate your competence in using systems, equipment and technology to deliver customer service (work-based product evidence)
- Identify customers' needs and how they have met those needs and provide evidence of how you have achieved this
- Provide evidence of dealing with challenging customers and conflict
- Provide evidence to show you are working effectively with others
- Provide evidence to show how you manage and are managing your own personal development

This evidence will need to be submitted via a showcase portfolio. The evidence contained in the showcase will be assessed by the EPA assessor against the following areas:

- Understanding the organisation
- Meeting regulations and legislation
- Systems and resources
- Product and service knowledge
- Influencing skills
- Personal organisation
- Dealing with customer conflict and challenge
- Developing self
- Being open to feedback
- Team working

Your showcase portfolio should be in a format in which it can be sent electronically, such as a word document, PowerPoint or PDF.

Alternatively, many EPA organisations will allow apprentices to produce a presentation, which could be video recorded and submitted along with copies of the presentation slides and notes as required.

It should take you around 10-12 hours to complete your showcase of evidence. It may take less time or longer to complete depending on how fast you work, any research required and how much you 'know your stuff'.

If you think it through, you will be likely to need at least 2 solid days to prepare your showcase, maybe more. Alternatively, you could work on it for 4 half days or for an hour each day for several days.

How you manage your time is up to you and your employer. Personally, I would start working on the knowledge questions first, get these out of the way and then begin collating the evidence of my behaviour and work performance, but how you work on it is a matter of personal preference. Just be prepared that you will have to put in fair amount of effort to get the result you are looking for.

You may use the internet for research in preparation for your showcase, but your work must be your own and evidence of plagiarism will mean that work submitted will not be accepted. Assessors now have some very clever tools to check for evidence of plagiarism!

It is good to look up theory and they work of others but always make sure that your work is original and personalised to you. This means that your work will always be authentic, and you can never be accused of copying. I know I have labored this point, but it really is a big one, so please take note.

A really quick way of researching information is by using Google Images. Sometimes Google Images will give you an idea of where to start if you don't understand something. That doesn't mean you should put them into your showcase but if you are struggling with an answer it can often provide a good visual clue.

If you opt to deliver your showcase by method of presentation, then slides should be submitted in advance to your personal tutor first to be checked over and then he/she will look to submit them in advance to the EPA organisation.

The apprentice showcase will normally be completed BEFORE any other stages of the end-point assessment. The EPA assessor will grade and report upon the outcome of the showcase. Some EPA centres will not give any feedback until all assessments have been completed.

Let's look at exactly what you need to put in to your showcase. If you look at each section step by step, then this will make the task of putting together your showcase easier. Make sure you cover EVERY outcome so that you maximise your chances of success. Remember that this EPA requires 100% pass mark, so you need to cover **everything** in your showcase.

Key words / Command Verbs

Take note of the key-words used in each question. It is important to understand the key words so that you know what your EPA assessor will be looking for when they are marking your work. The key words at the start of each question are known as 'command verbs'. They tell you what to do. There is a list of command verbs an explanation at the end of this section.

For example:

'Describe the types of customer(s) you deal with within your job role'.

You might respond with something like:

'Most of our customers are wealthy business people. They are generally looking for the best deal they can get as they shop around a lot. Our products are so expensive, and customers often buy in bulk because they then sell on the products they buy from us online and they want to make the best possible profit they can. They are often so busy that they don't want to chat much, and they want to get straight to the point of the sale so that they can get on and do the next thing they need to do. Some customers are a bit more friendly and take the time to make conversation a bit more, but typically, my customers are very busy people'.

A response like:

'Busy, rich people' would be insufficient. This is because the command verb 'describe' has not been met.

Putting your showcase together.

First of all – decide which format you are going to use. You can produce a word document, PowerPoint, handwritten document or video. The format doesn't really matter, it is the content that matters. However, some EPA centres might have their own rules about how they want it presented so always check before you start work as you wouldn't want to waste your time making a video, for example, which the EPA organisation won't accept.

Secondly - make a start, write a header, or something, anything. Tasks are always more daunting before you make a start on them.

I personally like presentations (like PowerPoint slides). They are quick to put together, easy to edit and to add pictures to if you want to. It is also nice because you can move the order of the slides round easily to make the showcase flow better. That way, if you write it in a random order, at least you can make it flow correctly afterwards without hours of copy and paste. But the choice is yours. Word documents are great too.

The main thing is to get started. If you are using PowerPoint as a format for presenting your showcase, that's fine, but unless you want to actually present (as in deliver a presentation to go with the slides) then you will need to make sure ALL the information is on the slides. If you are going to physically present as well as use slides, then you should bullet point only.

Make a cover first for your showcase. It doesn't need to be too complicated but something to give your EPA assessor a good first impression of your work.

Something simple, like the one below will do. You can add a date, your job role and the company name as well if you want to.

The photo below shows an example cover for a showcase, created using PowerPoint.

Ok, great, you have made a cover. It's a start and once you get started you might just get on a roll.

Now, pick a question that you already know the answer to. Write out the answer. It doesn't need to be in order, just yet, we need to get you on a roll.

Alternatively, you can work methodically from question 1 all the way to the end, whatever floats your boat! What you want to avoid though is stopping on a question if you find it a bit tricky. You can always contact your tutor for some support on anything you are struggling with.

To give you an idea of the standard of work, and detail, required, there is a sample answer shown below for you.

My Showcase

* I work as a customer service apprentice at Sales Are Us Ltd.
* Sales Are Us Ltd., sell spare parts for household appliances, like vacuum bags, door knobs for ovens, the glass shelves in fridges and so on.
* Its good because if you break something, you can probably repair it, things like washing machines, fridges and cookers are really expensive to replace so if you can repair them for a fraction of the cost, then this saves you lots of money.

Explain the difference between the features and benefits of products and/or services in relation to the organisation.

* So, the feature / benefit comparison would be this:

* Feature – spare parts to fix your appliance
* Benefit – saves you money so you can spend money on more interesting things than a new washing machine, such as that holiday you were saving for

* The features of a product are facts about it, so what it does, the benefits of a product are what it does for you or how it helps

Describe how to maintain knowledge of the organisation's products and/or services.

* I keep my knowledge up to date by:
* Attending training sessions each month on new products. This month was cooker door insert training, so we looked at how these work and how to sell them to customers
* I also check on the system each time I sell a product. I read out the product information to customers and so that helps me learn about which products are best when other customers call in and aren't sure what product they need
* I also look at the newsletter that comes round each day with new information on to help us with selling products to customers

As you can see, I have made it really clear to the EPA assessor which question I have answered by heading my slides with the question. That way, there is no doubt that I have answered it.

In the slide above I have given 3 different examples of ways in which I keep my knowledge of products up to date. This ensures that the marker, if they are not keen on my first answer, has others to consider and so I am confident I have covered everything in my answer and I will gain the marks needed to pass this element of the showcase.

Summary:

- Choose the format you are going to use for your showcase (PowerPoint/Word document)
- Get started & make a cover page to inspire you

- Begin working through each of the questions and requirements in each of the sections below
- Check you have answered every outcome and requirement against the assessment plan
- Show your manager/tutor/friend or anyone who has the patience to read and check it for you to look to see if you have missed anything
- Make sure your work is your own and your **answers relate to your own job role** and industry
- Never copy and paste from the internet. Assessors have clever ways of checking for this and your work is highly likely to be rejected if you do.

Knowledge questions to answer in your showcase.

There **are only 14 questions** including the distinction questions.

Give the distinction questions a try if you can. Then look at the behaviours you need to showcase afterwards.

SHOWCASE KNOWLEDGE QUESTIONS:

Prepare CLEAR AND DETAILED WRITTEN RESPONSES TO THE 14 QUESTIONS BELOW:
(UNLESS YOU ARE DOING AN ORAL PRESENATATION and in that case then prepare notes or presentation slides)

Tick off when done	The main question you need to answer is in this column	When you are putting your answer together, also look to answer these related questions. Answering these will help ensure you cover all areas of the question and don't miss anything.
1	Explain the use of different systems, equipment and/or technology available in the organisation to meet customer needs effectively	What are the systems, equipment and/or technology your organisation uses to effectively meet customer needs? In your role how would you use the systems, equipment and/or technology to support customer needs?
2	Describe the measures and evaluation tools used in the organisation to monitor customer service levels	What are the types of measurement used to monitor customer service levels? What are the types of evaluation tool used to monitor customer service levels?
3	State the aims of the organisation in relation to its sector AND state what is meant by the organisation's 'brand promise'	What is the difference between public, private and third sector organisation? What is your organisation business type and purpose? What does 'brand promise' mean?
4	Explain how the organisation's core values relate to its service culture	What is meant by an organisations core value? What are your organisations core values? What is meant by service culture? What is your

		organisations service culture? How does your organisations core values link to the service culture?
5	State the purpose of different organisational policies and procedures that affect their customer service role	What is the purpose of an organisational policy? List the organisational policies and procedures that could affect a customer service role. What should be included in a complaints process or procedure?
6	Describe the type of guidelines in a digital media policy that affect the use of social and digital media in the work environment.	What is meant by digital media? What digital media policies exist in customer service organisations?
7	OPTIONAL: DISTINCTION QUESTION: Explain how the organisational policies and procedures impact on the delivery of customer service	THIS IS A DISTINCTION QUESTION AND THERE IS NO ADDITIONAL GUIDANCE TO BREAK DOWN THE QUESTION
8	Explain how the relevant legislation and regulations affect the organisation's customer service provision	Identify appropriate legislation and regulation and how this effects your organisation.
9	State the responsibilities of employees and employers under the Health and Safety at Work Act	Why is it important to keep information confidential within an organisation? What information needs to be kept and remain confidential within your organisation? What are the responsibilities of

		the *employee* under the health and safety at work act? What are the responsibilities of the *employer* under the health and safety at work act?
10	OPTIONAL DISTINCTION QUESTION: Explain the potential impact on the organisation if it fails to adhere to each of the relevant legislation and regulations.	THIS IS A DISTINCTION QUESTION AND THERE IS NO ADDITIONAL GUIDANCE TO BREAK DOWN THE QUESTION
11	OPTIONAL DISTINCTION QUESTION: Explain how a code of practice or ethical standards affects customer service	THIS IS A DISTINCTION QUESTION AND THERE IS NO ADDITIONAL GUIDANCE TO BREAK DOWN THE QUESTION
12	Explain the difference between the features and benefits of products and/or services in relation to the organisation.	What are your organisations products and/or services? What is the difference between providing a product and providing a service?
13	Describe how to maintain your knowledge of the organisation's products and/or services.	How do you update and maintain your knowledge of your organisation's products and/or services?
14	OPTIONAL DISTINCTION QUESTION: Explain why it is important to update your knowledge of the organisation's products and/or services.	THIS IS A DISTINCTION QUESTION AND THERE IS NO ADDITIONAL

		GUIDANCE TO BREAK DOWN THE QUESTION

Tick off each of the number boxes to show that you have answered the questions.

Now let's look at the behaviours you need to show in the showcase.

In order to demonstrate your behaviours through your showcase you will need to produce evidence.

Have a discussion with your tutor about which evidence would be most suitable for your showcase. Some evidence ideas have been listed for you in the table below.

When you submit evidence for your showcase, please annotate it to show what it covers and the context the evidence came from.

Remember that your EPA assessor doesn't know your job role or procedures. You may think you're stating the obvious when you write what a piece of evidence is but it may not be obvious to an outsider to your company or industry.

	WHAT YOU NEED TO SHOW YOU HAVE DONE	EVIDENCE IDEAS
1	Identify customer needs: **Offer** appropriate product and/or service options to meet the identified needs of customers and the needs of the organisation.	CUSTOMER ORDER FORMS
2	Offer product and/or service options to customers in a logical and reasoned manner. Clearly explain how options offered meet the customer needs. **Communicate** to customers in a clear and coherent manner how the products and/or	FEEDBACK FROM CUSTOMERS, WITNESS REPORTS, REFLECTIVE ACCOUNT SIGNED BY MANAGER TO CONFIRM

	services meet their needs.	
3	Handle customer objections in a positive and professional manner. **Handle** customer objections in a positive and professional manner	FEEDBACK FROM CUSTOMERS, WITNESS REPORTS, REFLECTIVE ACCOUNT SIGNED BY MANAGER TO CONFIRM
4	**DISTINCTION: Provide** appropriate explanations to customers in situations where a mutually beneficial outcome cannot be reached.	FEEDBACK FROM CUSTOMERS, WITNESS REPORTS, REFLECTIVE ACCOUNT SIGNED BY MANAGER TO CONFIRM / CUSTOMER EMAILS / ACCOUNT NOTES
5	Agree goals and deadlines for completing tasks with an appropriate person. Prioritise and plan the completion of tasks to meet delivery deadlines. **Prioritise and plan** the completion of tasks according to agreed deadlines.	PERFORMANCE REVIEWS / TO DO LISTS / EMAILS SHOWING WORK COMPLETED ON TIME
6	Use tools and techniques to monitor progress of tasks. Monitor and adjust priorities as required. Meet agreed deadlines. **Use** appropriate tools and techniques to monitor the progress of tasks completion.	PERFORMANCE REVIEWS / TO DO LISTS EMAILS SHOWING WORK COMPLETED ON TIME
7	**DISTINCTION: Respond** in a professional manner to challenges and changes and adjust priorities accordingly.	PERFORMANCE REVIEWS / WITNESS REPORTS
8	Show patience, calmness and empathy when dealing with challenging customer situations. Use active listening skills when communicating with customers. Use appropriate questioning skills. **Maintain** calm and patience at all times when dealing with challenging customer situations.	WITNESS REPORTS / PERFOMANCE APPRAISALS / CUSTOMER FEEDBACK
9	Show understanding of the customer view point. **Demonstrate** sensitivity to, and interest in, the customers' concerns.	WITNESS REPORTS / PERFOMANCE APPRAISALS / CUSTOMER FEEDBACK / TRANSCRIPTS OF CUSTOMER CALLS
10	Explain the next steps and/or customer options in a logical manner. **Communicate** in a clear and coherent manner the next steps and/or options to meet the needs and expectations of customers.	WITNESS REPORTS / PERFOMANCE APPRAISALS / CUSTOMER FEEDBACK / TRANSCRIPTS OF CUSTOMER CALLS
11	Provide clear sign-posting or resolution to meet customers' needs and manage customer expectations. Deal with and resolve the customer conflict or challenge presented in line with	WITNESS REPORTS / PERFOMANCE APPRAISALS / CUSTOMER FEEDBACK / TRANSCRIPTS OF

	organisational and/or policies procedure.	CUSTOMER CALLS / NOTES ON CUSTOMER ACCOUNTS
12	Keep customers informed of progress while resolving issues.	WITNESS REPORTS / PERFOMANCE APPRAISALS / CUSTOMER FEEDBACK / TRANSCRIPTS OF CUSTOMER CALLS / NOTES ON CUSTOMER ACCOUNTS
13	**Maintain** accurate records of customer issues and progress to resolution	CUSTOMER ACCOUNT RECORDS / WITNESS REPORTS
14	DISTINCTION: **Take ownership** of customer issues, taking the appropriate actions to ensure customers' needs and expectations are met.	CUSTOMER ACCOUNT RECORDS / WITNESS REPORTS
15	**Identify** own strengths and weaknesses in relation to working within a customer service role. **Apply** the techniques of self-assessment to look at own strengths and weaknesses. **Conduct** a self-assessment to identify own strengths and weaknesses in relation to the job role.	SELF ASSESSMENT ACTIVITIES / ANALYSE OWN STRENGTHS, WEAKNESSES, OPPORTUNITES AND THREATS (SWOT ANALYSIS) PERFORMANCE REVIEWS
16	**Prepare a personal development plan** that helps to achieve personal goals and development needs. **Review and update** your personal development plan. The personal development plan should support the achievement of agreed learning and development goals.	PERSONAL DEVELOPMENT PLAN (LOOK FOR ONE ONLINE TO GIVE YOU IDEAS THEN ADAPT. UPDATE IT AS YOU GO THROUGH THE PROCESS).
17	DISTINCTION: Review the effectiveness of their personal development plan and update it accordingly.	PRODUCE A WRITTEN PIECE OF WORK REVIEWING YOUR PDP AND SHOW THE CHANGES YOU HAVE MADE AS A RESULT OF THE REVIEW.
18	Identify suitable ways of obtaining informal and formal feedback from others. Obtain useful and constructive feedback about your own service skills and knowledge from others. Seek constructive feedback about their customer service skills and knowledge from others	CUSTOMER FEEDBACK / ONLINE REVIEWS (THAT RELATE TO YOU DIRECTLY) / WITNESS REPORTS
19	Positively respond to all feedback. Use the feedback received to take responsibility for maintaining and developing your personal customer service skills and knowledge. Use feedback from others to develop own customer	PERFORMANCE APPRAISALS / WITNESS REPORTS / REFLECTIVE ACCOUNT

	service skills and knowledge.	
20	Demonstrate the interpersonal skills required to work effectively as part of a team. Work with others in a positive and productive manner.	EMAILS TO COLLEAGUES / MEETING MINUTES / WITNESS REPORTS
21	Communicate consistently with team members in the interest of helping customers. Demonstrate cooperation when working with others. Communicate information in a timely and reliable manner to team members to support them in meeting customer needs efficiently	EMAILS TO COLLEAGUES / MEETING MINUTES / WITNESS REPORTS / PERFORMANCE APPRAISAL
22	DISTINCTION: Recognise when to adapt personal behaviours and communication approach to meet the needs of team members and customers	EMAILS TO COLLEAGUES / MEETING MINUTES / WITNESS REPORTS / PERFORMANCE APPRAISAL
23	Share personal learning with others to support good practice. Present your ideas and recommendations for improvements in customer service to others.	EMAILS TO COLLEAGUES / MEETING MINUTES / WITNESS REPORTS / PERFORMANCE APPRAISAL / PROJECT WORK
24	DISTINCTION: Present reasoned ideas for improving customer service practice to the appropriate colleagues	EMAILS TO COLLEAGUES / MEETING MINUTES / WITNESS REPORTS / PERFORMANCE APPRAISAL / PROJECT WORK

EXAMPLE EVIDENCE

Below is a little more detail about some of the evidence types to help you prepare for your showcase. You should be used to gathering evidence by now. If you have any queries, have a chat with your personal tutor.

Witness reports	*Show your manager the table of information above. Ask him/her to write a statement to show how you have met each criteria, giving examples of how you have done it.*
Performance appraisals	*You should get plenty of feedback as an apprentice and some of this*

	should be documented. You might be able to use it to meet the criteria above. Read it through, photocopy and highlight which areas you think it could meet for you.
Emails	*Emails are great evidence of you dealing with customers and can show the good work you have done. You should add some notes to emails to give some context to the email so that your EPA assessor understands what you did*
Meeting minutes	*These are only useful if you are directly mentioned in them and they clearly state how you have met the criteria.*
Customer feedback	*You can either create your own feedback survey or collect ones your company already use. Have a look to see which criteria they meet.*

Have a look at the piece of evidence shown below.

This is a letter from a customer thanking a customer service practitioner (in this case, James) for his help.

Which of the criteria above do you think a piece of evidence like this could help James with if he was to use it in his showcase?

Dear James,

Thankyou so much for helping me today to choose an air conditioning unit for our house. It was good to see the range of options available to us. You were really helpful. Thankyou so much.

Joseph Black

So, this meets outcome 1 as it shows that James clearly identified the customer needs. Also 2 has been met as James showed the customer a range of options and the customer was happy about it. Outcome 2 has been met because James showed a range of options. Outcome 3 has not been met because the letter does not show that James overcame any objections.

If you are using evidence of this type, then try to authenticate it. Essentially, anyone could write a letter like this, and so to show it is genuine, you could attach a copy of a receipt to show what the customer ordered or ask your manager to sign it as a witness.

Don't worry if your evidence is not 'perfect' looking. Naturally occurring evidence won't be perfect. Like the letter above, it may not be professionally produced, and a lot of customer feedback might be on a note, or a thankyou card. It doesn't mean you can't use it. Authenticity of evidence is important, so you might need to add notes to explain the context behind the evidence.

Other excellent sources of evidence are feedback forms filled in by customers, or social media review (e.g. Facebook, trip advisor), but to use these they would have to specifically mention your name.

A good idea would be to create a customer survey (if your company don't use these already). You can then use this as evidence to show you have met the criteria. Surveys are easy to create using Microsoft Word. Simply go into Word, click 'file' and then 'new'. You will then see this screen:

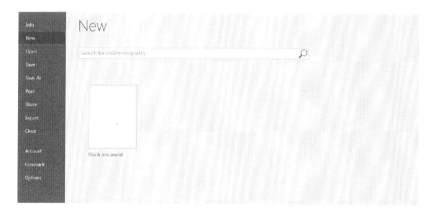

Then simply type the word 'survey' and you will be given options as to which type of survey you want to use. You can then word the questions you want to ask your customers to suit the requirements of your showcase. Then simply hand out to customers and once you have responses, you can take photos and upload them to your showcase document. An example customer survey, created on a word document is on the next page.

Systems and versions of Microsoft Word can vary, so have a look online for instructions if you are not sure or if your system works differently.

[Company Name]

How are we doing?

We are committed to providing you with the best dining experience possible, so we welcome your comments. Please fill out this questionnaire and place it in the box in our lobby. Thank you.

Please rate the quality of the service you received from your server

☐ 1 ☐ 2 ☐ 3 ☐ 4 ☐ 5

Disappointing   Exceptional

How well did your server identify and meet your needs?

☐ 1 ☐ 2 ☐ 3 ☐ 4 ☐ 5

Disappointing   Exceptional

Please rate the quality of your entree.

☐ 1 ☐ 2 ☐ 3 ☐ 4 ☐ 5

Disappointing   Exceptional

Were you offered a range of services or alternative products?

☐ 1 ☐ 2 ☐ 3 ☐ 4 ☐ 5

Disappointing   Exceptional

How sell did your server listen to your needs and meet your expectations?

☐ 1 ☐ 2 ☐ 3 ☐ 4 ☐ 5

Disappointing   Exceptional

Please rate your overall dining experience.

☐ 1 ☐ 2 ☐ 3 ☐ 4 ☐ 5

Disappointing   Exceptional

What was the name of your server?   /   Customer name/date/signature

Example witness statement:

Have a look to see which of the criteria you think this witness statement meets.

FAO End Point Assessment Organisation

From Dan Charles, Team Leader at XDN Group.

Telephone: xxxxxx   Email Dan.charles@xdngroup.co.uk

Regarding – Paul Warner – Customer Service Practitioner Apprentice.

Paul has worked within my team as a customer service apprentice for the past 12 months. Paul works in the call centre, dealing with customer requests to book in engineers to repair household appliances, such as cookers or fridges.

Paul knows to prioritise the phone lines, as if we don't answer timely then we lose business. In between calls, Paul makes sure that he follows up any complicated customer queries or sends in reports we have asked for.

Paul is consistent at sending in reports on time and he keeps a spreadsheet to record all the bookings and payments he has made each day. He also keeps a to-do list, which helps him to keep track of his tasks for the day and he shows me this and lets me know if there are any tasks remaining, for example, if he is waiting news from another department and so has to follow up the next day. Paul is an excellent and valued member of the team and has a fantastic rapport with customers. He often looks to sell additional services to customers, such as insurance products.

Top tips when asking for witness statements:

- Ask the witness to look at the assessment plan (or the list of criteria above) so they know exactly what the EPA assessor will be looking for

- Make sure it gives their contact details for authenticity (full name, job title, relationship to you as the apprentice & phone number)
- Ask the witness to give examples of what you do in your day to day tasks
- Use the assessment plan (and/or list above) yourself to tick off exactly what the witness testimony meets so that you know what other criteria you will need to meet from other evidence.
- Show your tutor and ask them for feedback and see if they agree with the criteria you think it meets.
- Offer to make the witness a cup of tea or coffee while they write it, managers can be very busy people, let them see that you might be saving them time!

Other ideas:

- Take a photo of your to-do list or system scheduler.
- screen shot customer service entries from your IT system.
- Always check that you are permitted to use evidence and you are not breaking any data protection rules or GDPR guidance.

Checking and proof-reading your work

Once you are confident that your answers make sense and you have met all of the criteria, then spellcheck/grammar check your work. If you have used a word document to prepare your showcase, you could even listen to it to make certain that it flows ok. To do this, in a word document, click 'view', then click 'read mode', then click 'view' again, and 'read aloud'. There will then be a 'play' icon at the upper right-hand side of the screen. Different versions of Word may vary the commands, so just Google it if you have any issues. This is a great new tool for proof-reading and checking your own work.

Put your work away for a day or so and then check it over with fresh eyes. The pass and distinction criteria are a bit like the mark scheme, so you can see exactly what the EPA assessor will be marking your work against, by reviewing the criteria. Reflect on your own work yourself, as if it was someone else's work and you were marking it. Would you realistically award the mark? This will give you a good idea of how you will do when your work is marked and give you a good basis on which to make any changes before you hand it in.

Next, go to the website which shows the assessment plan for your apprenticeship standard which is shown below. Check that your showcase meets all the requirements and that you have not missed anything.

https://www.instituteforapprenticeships.org/media/1166/customer_service_practitioner.pdf

If you are planning on verbally presenting your presentation slides to the EPA assessor, then you will need to practice this. You could practice the delivery of your showcase to colleagues, friends, your tutor or your manager. You could even practice it alone. If you are really confident, you could video record or voice record your presentation and watch it to give yourself ideas on how to improve when it comes to the real thing. You will need to send your presentation slides into the EPA in advance and arrange a date/time for the live presentation. Specifics of how this will be arranged can vary between EPA centres and how they chose to organise assessments, so please check with them or ask your personal tutor to make enquiries for you.

If you are now happy with your showcase, then show it to your tutor/assessor to look over. They will then liaise with the EPA organisation in order to get this submitted and marked for you.

Most EPA organisations will get the results over to you within around 14 working days, but service levels vary between organisations, so if in doubt, ask your tutor or contact your EPA organisation.

Once the showcase has been submitted you can now look at preparing for the next two stages of your EPA.

Apprentice showcase key features:

- This is the first thing the EPA assessor will see and will use this to 'get to know you and your skills/knowledge

- Can be showcased through delivery of a presentation or by a virtual form of assessment such as a report, storyboard or journal or word document
- Weighted at 65% of the EPA
- A chance to show off skills and the application of knowledge
- 100% of all the pass criteria to achieve a pass
- 100 % of the pass criteria PLUS 70% of the distinction criteria to achieve a distinction.
- Remember to add lots of evidence to demonstrate the fantastic work you have done whilst on your apprenticeship
- Attempt every single outcome. Do not miss one out, it is 100% pass mark, double and triple check that you have covered everything you need to
- Attempt all of the distinction criteria if you can

Top Tips:

- Make your showcase short – about 12-15 pages long – but full of excellent evidence
- Some EPA centres will have specific rules about how long it should be, some don't
- Read, read and read again the assessment plan, then take it to your manager to read and ask him/her to write a detailed witness statement about your work and how you have met the standards
- Make sure not to miss out any of the criteria needed

- Use customer feedback surveys or similar evidence
- Check you have met the command verbs when answering questions (command verbs are the words at the start of questions that tell you what to do)

Use of command verbs

When you are putting together your showcase, take into consideration the command verbs below:

Command Verb	Requirement
Explain	Clarify a topic by giving a detailed account as to how and why it occurs, or what is meant by the use of this term in a particular context. The writing should have clarity so that complex procedures or sequences of events can be understood, defining key terms where appropriate, and be substantiated with relevant research. This should be sentences rather than bullet points.
Describe	Provide a detailed explanation as to how or why something happens. This should be sentences rather than bullet points. It should be clear that you understand the topic.
State	To specify in clear terms the key aspects pertaining to a topic without being overly descriptive. Refer to evidence and examples where appropriate. This can be a list rather than full sentences.
Offer	This is a behavioural command verb for which evidence should be seen to confirm that an offer has been made to the customer in the appropriate context

List	A simple list, does not have to be a written sentence and bullet points are acceptable
Communicate	This is a behavioural command verb for which evidence should be seen to confirm that suitable communication has been achieved.
Handle	This is a behavioural command verb and suitable evidence should be seen to show that the apprentice has been able to deal with (handle) the situation appropriately. It should be clear as to the context of the situation.
Demonstrate	This is a behavioural command verb and apprentices' work should show that a particular aspect has been seen
Conduct	This is a behavioural command verb and suitable evidence should be seen to show that the apprentice's behaviour is appropriate.
General Behavioural Questions	Any questions that require you to demonstrate skills/competencies and behaviours must be met with suitable evidence that is reliable, valid and sufficient to show competence in this area. This could be evidenced by: - Work-based product evidence - Video evidence - Learning journals (for feedback section) - Performance appraisals - Other suitable evidence

This is a guide only and should be used to help you prepare for your End Point Assessment. It is HIGHLY recommended that you read the assessment plan for this apprenticeship standard, which can be found online. Also, please check the criteria and information sent to you by the EPA centre you will be assessed by.

https://www.instituteforapprenticeships.org/apprenticeship-standards/customer-service-practitioner/

USEFUL WEBSITES FOR FURTHER INFORMATION

ACAS Employment Rights Helpline
http://www.acas.org.uk/index.aspx?articleid=4489

All about school leavers
https://www.allaboutschoolleavers.co.uk/articles/article/235/how-to-find-a-list-of-all-the-apprenticeships-available

Amazing Apprenticeships
https://twitter.com/AmazingAppsUK

Apprenticeship EPA Centre

www.apprenticeship-centre.co.uk/EPA or
Telephone 0845 22 5020 email
info@apprenticeship-centre.co.uk

Apprenticeship Helpline
Nationalhelpdesk@apprenticeships.gov.uk or
Telephone 0800 015 0400

Apprenticeships in Wales
http://gov.wales/topics/educationandskills/skillsandtr

aining/apprenticeships/?lang=en

BKSB Functional Skills Online Training
https://www.bksb.co.uk/

Customer Service Practitioner assessment plan
https://www.instituteforapprenticeships.org/media/1166/customer_service_practitioner.pdf

Customer Service Practitioner apprenticeship standard
https://www.instituteforapprenticeships.org/apprenticeship-standards/customer-service-practitioner/

ESFA
https://www.gov.uk/government/organisations/education-and-skills-funding-agency

ForSkills Functional Skills Online Training
http://www.forskills.co.uk/

Further Education and Skills Apprenticeships
https://www.gov.uk/topic/further-education-skills/apprenticeships

Get in, Go Far Government Apprenticeship Website
https://www.getingofar.gov.uk/

Institute of Customer Services
https://www.instituteofcustomerservice.com/

National Apprenticeship Service
https://www.gov.uk/apply-apprenticeship

Pearson Past Papers for Functional Skills
http://qualifications.pearson.com/en/support/support-topics/exams/past-papers.html

Prospects career advice

https://www.prospects.ac.uk/

Register of Apprenticeship Training Providers
https://www.gov.uk/guidance/register-of-apprenticeship-training-providers

The Apprenticeship Centre Facebook Page
https://www.facebook.com/TheApprenticeshipCentreBirmingham/

The Apprenticeship Centre
http://www.apprenticeship-centre.co.uk/

The Apprenticeship Levy
https://www.gov.uk/government/publications/apprenticeship-levy-how-it-will-work/apprenticeship-levy-how-it-will-work

The Ask Project
https://amazingapprenticeships.com/

The Institute for Apprenticeships
https://www.instituteforapprenticeships.org/

ABOUT THE AUTHOR

 Louise Webber studied Psychology and Philosophy at The University of Liverpool. She then went on to study Management at Postgraduate Level.

Louise worked for three major banking institutions at management level and was very successful at meeting targets and audit requirements.

Louise went on to work in the education sector, working in both mainstream and special needs schools. She re-trained to work within the adult education sector and studied to become a tutor/assessor for NVQ and Apprenticeships then becoming Lead Internal Verifier within a training centre. Louise now works as Head of Apprenticeships and Head of End Point Assessment, responsible for the success of the Apprenticeship schemes, staff training and development, recruitment and quality management as well as being the Ofsted nominee for the centre.

Louise successfully applied via the tender process in 2018 for registration for her centre for status as an End Point Assessment Organisation who are registered on the Register of End Point Assessment Organisations (RoEPAO) as Apprenticeship EPA Centre.

Louise manages a team of End Point Assessors, internally verifies work and ensures processes and procedures are in place to meet the requirements of audit and compliance.

Louise has supported her team of tutors to successfully complete over 2000 Apprenticeship and NVQ courses for learners within the training centre where she works. In addition, Louise has worked as a Standards Verifier for the world's largest examination board, supporting other centres to achieve high standards for learners and success within the education sector.

Apprenticeship EPA Centre can be contacted on 0845 223 5020.

www.apprenticeship-centre.co.uk/epa

Louise has also worked with other end point assessment centres to support apprentices in preparation for their EPA and has written examination material for Apprenticeship EPA Centre.

Louise is the author of a guide book for those interested in (or already on) apprenticeship courses:

'Apprenticeships: A Guide for Students and Parents', written in 2018 and also available on Amazon:

https://www.amazon.co.uk/Apprenticeships-Students-Parents-Louise-Webber/dp/1980411689/ref=sr_1_1?s=books&ie=UTF8&qid=153338238 3&sr=1-1&keywords=apprenticeships

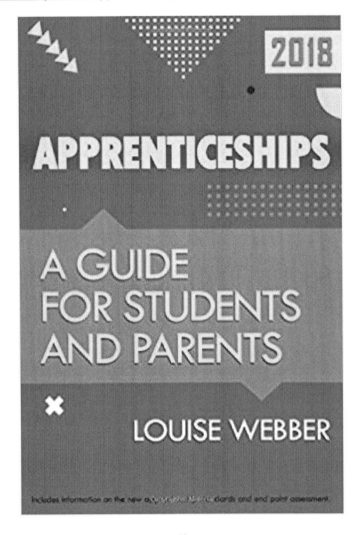

Apprenticeship End Point
Assessment Success

CUSTOMER
SERVICE
PRACTITIONER

EPA

All the information you need
to pass or gain a distinction
grade.

LOUISE WEBBER

THE FULL GUIDE TO EPA FOR THE CUSTOMER SERVICE PRACTITONER EPA

The author has also published a full guide to the EPA for this apprenticeship, which includes all the information you have read here, as well as more detail about EPA, as well as details of how to prepare for the other two areas of the EPA for this apprenticeship. This book is also available on Amazon.

https://www.amazon.co.uk/Apprenticeship-End-Point-Assessment-Success-ebook/dp/B07H8KDSB8/ref=sr_1_2?ie=UTF8&qid=1549225391&sr=8-2&keywords=louise+webber

DISCLAIMER

Every effort has been made to ensure the currency, validity and accuracy of information contained within this book, however the publisher, author and editor cannot be held responsible for any errors or omissions, however caused.

No responsibility for loss or damage occasioned by any person acting or otherwise, as a result of information contained within this book, can be accepted by the author, editor or publisher.

This book was published independently of The Apprenticeship Centre and Apprenticeship EPA Centre and associated businesses.

Centre processes may vary. EPAO centres use their own systems of grading work and whilst this guide is there to support you, it cannot comprehensively cover every eventuality of questioning and/or formatting of end point assessment as each end point assessment centre have been tasked by the ESFA to create their own mark scheme and resources.

FIRST PUBLISHING DATE

This book was first published in February 2019.

Copyright: 2019 Louise Webber

REGISTER OF END POINT ASSESSMENT ORGANISATIONS

The register of end point assessment organisations details all the companies that offer EPA. Click the link below then follow the prompts for more information.

https://www.gov.uk/guidance/register-of-end-point-assessment-organisations

To check for the most up to date information on available Apprenticeship standards go to
https://www.gov.uk/government/publications/apprenticeship-standards-list-of-occupations-available--2

Printed in Great Britain
by Amazon